An Outline of Confucianism

An Outline of Confucianism

Traditional and neoconfucianism,
and criticism

Don Y. Lee

Revised Edition

Eastern Press
Bloomington, IN
1988

EASTERN PRESS
426 East Sixth Street
Bloomington, Indiana 47401

Library of Congress Catalog Card Number:87-82510
International Standard Book Number:0-939758-16-4

Printed in the United States of America

CONTENTS

I *INTRODUCTION*

Confucius (552-479 B.C.),[1] the father
of Confucionism, was born in the state of
Lu (魯),[2] which is now the province of
Shan-Tung in the late part of the Spring-
Autumn period. His family name was Kung
(孔) and the first name was Ku (丘),
but in East Asia the family name always
comes first, thus Kung Ku was his whole
name. His pen name was Chung-Ni (仲尼).
His father was Kung Ho (孔 紇) and his
mother was Yen Cheng-Tsai (顏 徵 在).
His father passed away when Confucius was
three years old, so he grew up under poor
conditions. However, Confucius himself
mentioned that he began to study at the
age of fifteen, and became a man at his

---

[1]Some source indicates the birth-
date 551.

[2]This place is 昌 平 鄉 陬 邑 in
the State of Lu at that time.
史記,世家,第 十七(孔子世家).

thirtieth year.[1] Thereafter, he became
an inferior official, but he was gradually recognized by his superiors and finally became a Ta Ssu-K'ou (大 司 寇), an
equivalent position to the minister of
crime. This was the time that the social
order was chaotic, and in the state of Lu,
the three Chia-lao (三 家 老) were holding the practical political power in the
government. Confucius' idea while he was
in the office was to reduce the practical
political power of the three Cha-lao
(家 老) in order to bring the power
back to the ruler, Chou-Kung (周 公)
who was the founder of the state of Lu,
in order to recover an ordered and culti-
vated society just like the beginning of
the Chou dynasty. Nevertheless, he had
to leave the office after the several
years that he had held the position at
the age of fifty-six, because of idealog-
ical difference between the Chia-lao and
Confucius himself. Thereafter he began
to travel around with his deciples, not

---

[1] 吾 十 有 五.

only in the state of Lu, but also to other
states in China to teach his way to the
kings and the local lords for the social
order and peace. The overview of his
idea in his teaching was ethical didacti-
cismwith the care of Jen (a deep broad
love)[1] and Li (propriety) to produce
real gentlemen known as Chün-tzu (君 子).
who in turn govern their countries with
the idea of Jen and Li, then the world
under heaven would be in peace and pros-
perity.

With the main idea of Jen and Li in
his teachings, Confucius, along with his
desciples traveled around for fourteen
years, but the lords and states were
fighting more and more among themselves.
Thus the result of Confucius' teaching
was not realized in making the societies

---

[1]For the precise meaning of Jen,
there are different opinions. However,
it refers to a further deep love than
the love in English language.

peaceful and ordered. With a deep sigh,
Confucius returned to his native state of
Lu at the age of 70.[1] At this time, his
son Li (鯉) who had reached 50 in his
age, passed away, also his beloved disciple Yen Hui (顏 回), who was 30 years
younger than Confucius, passed away.
Following Yen Hui's death, Tzu Lu (子 路),
another beloved disciple also passed away;
the good all died young. Confucius was
also sick in the same year, thus he suf-
fered a lot.

From this time on, Confucius concen-
trated on educating his disciples and upon
compiling the classics such as The Book
of Poetry, The Book of History, and the
Spring-Autumn Annals.

In a word, Confucius used the term
"Heaven." This means that Confucanism
maintains a reticence before a supernatural being, so it does have a deep
spiritual and religious value. However,
it is not religion, but ethical didacti-
cism for the society and for the govern-

---

[1]Some documents show 69 instead of 70.

ment.

    After all, the purpose of this work
is to respond to the intellectuals' question about what the difference between
traditional and Neo-Confucianism is, and
why Confucianism is criticized in the
modern period.

The Basic Principle

    Above, I have indicated that Confu-
cius' central concept is Jen, a deep
love. He was a humanistic philosopher
and educator. In this introduction I
will be concerned with T'ien (天),
Chün-tzu (君 子), and Jen (仁).

1. T'ien (Heaven, 天).
    The grandson of Confucius, Tzu-Ssu
(子 思) said, "Heaven and man unite"
(天 人 合 一). Here one can notice that
Confucianism is in accordance with cosmology. Heaven and man together build a
heavenly, peaceful order on earth. In
China, however the systematized ideas

began from Confucius. In this regard,
Confucius' systematized ideas were also
based upon the previous works. In the
case of the T'ien (天) concept in the
preconfucian period, the Chinese people
believed that Heaven gave birth to people. Therefore, the ancient people believed that their greatest ancester is
Heaven. The following passage is from
Meng-tzu (孟 子):

> 天之生此民也．使先知覺後知，
> 使先覺覺後覺也．[1]
>
> *In Heaven's production of man-*
> *kind, it is to let those who*
> *know first should instruct the*
> *later, and those who understand*
> *first should make the later*
> *understand.*

Thus, Heaven is a supernatural being and
religious object. The ancient people
also believed that Heaven governs the
people through the ruler. In this connection the ruler who is known as 上帝 ，

---

[1] 孟子．萬章章句上，第七章．五節．

became an identical term in China. This
concept was generated to Confucius, and
Confucius himself often used the term
T'ien. For example, when his beloved
disciple Yen-Hui (顏　回) died the
70 year old sage cried loudly, saying
that "Heaven destroyed me, Heaven destroyed me!" as follows:

顏回死, 子曰, 噫, 天喪予,
天喪予.[1]

Tr: *Yen Hui died. Confucius said*
Oh, Heaven destroyed me, Heaven
destroyed me.

Here, one can see that Confucius used
the term T'ien as a supernatural being.

Furthering the meaning of T'ien, I
have come to present Tung Chung-shu (董
仲舒), the greatest Confucian scholar
in the Han dynasty period. According to
Tung Chung-shu, T'ien is expounded as
follows:

A. T'ien is the origin of everything.
B. Human is the most superior of
    everything.

---

[1] 論語, 先進, 第十一第八章.

  C. T'ien and human are similar.
  D. Ruler (king) is appointed by T'ien.
  E. The sign (tally) of being appoint-
      ed by T'ien (受 命 之 符).
  F. The ruler (king) follows Heavenly
      laws and holds them in esteem.
  G. Ruler sacrifices to Heaven.
  H. Reward and punishment.

a. T'ien is the origin of everything.
According to Tung Chung-shu (董 仲 舒),
one was born from his or her parents, the
parents were born from the great parents,
and the great parents were born from the
great-great parents. Thus, if one traces
back to the very ultimate, one reaches to
the Heaven. In this regard, according to
Tung Chung-shu, Heaven is the greatest
ancester. Here, the idea is that Heaven
is not only the greatest ancester for human, but also the greatest ancester for
everything in terms of the great nature.

b. Human is the most superior of everything. Tung Chung-shu asserted that
everything in the world is flourishing
because of nourishing human. In this,

human holds the highest superiority of
everything.

c. T'ien (Heaven) and humans are similar. This means that everything is born
from Heaven in the very origin. But human is the closest to heaven, therefore,
Heaven and human are similar in terms of
one's body as well as feeling, and so
forth. (For the relationship between
human and cosmology, see Chinese Eulogy
and Its Textual Variation by Don Y. Lee,
1983).

d. The ruler is appointed by T'ien.
Tung Chung-shu asserted that the ruler
is the one who is appointed by T'ien as
the ruler of the people.

受命之君, 天之所大顯也

*The ruler who is appointed [by
Heaven] is the manifestation of
Heaven.*

e. The sign (tally) of being appointed
by T'ien. This means how one knows who
will be appointed by Heaven as the

ruler. Tung Chung -shu's idea is that it
is not through human power to become a
ruler, but it is through natural arrival.
In other words, if there is a man whom
all the people respect in their hearts
and obey just as children obey their
parents, then there will be a happy omen
（天 瑞) to arrive to him.

f. The ruler follows the Heavenly laws
and holds them in esteem.

臣聞天之所大奉使之王者，必有
非人力所能致．而自至者，此受命
之符也。天下之人，同心歸之，
若歸父母，故天瑞應誠而至.[1]

Tr. *I heard that the ruler who is*
commissioned by Heaven is certain-
ly not the result of man power,
but he is the one that is the
natural arrival. [An ordinance
of Heaven].

g. Ruler sacrifices to Heaven. Tung-
Chung-shu's idea is that Heaven is King

---

[1] 賢良對策一．

of hundred gods, and the ruler holds the
highest esteem on Heaven.

天者百神之君也，王者之所最尊也[1]

Tr. *Heaven is the master of the hundred
gods, and to Heaven the ruler holds
the highest esteem.*

h.   Reward and punishment.   Tung Chung-
shu mentioned that Heaven appoints a high
gentleman as the ruler in order to rule
the people.   Therefore if the virtue is
sufficient for the people, then it is alright to be ruler.   On the other hand,
if the virtue is not sufficient and dis-
turbs the people, then Heaven removes
the rulership.

天之生民，非為王也，而天立王，
以為民也，故其德足以安樂民者，
天予之，其惡足以殘害民者，天奪之。

Tr. *It is not for ruler that Heaven
produces the people.   But Heaven
establishes ruler for the people.
Therefore, if the virtue of the
ruler is sufficient to pacify
the people, then Heaven confers*

----

[1] 春秋繁露，郊義茅之十之。

him.   If the virtue is not
sufficient enough and harm-
ful to the people, then Heaven
takes away his rulership.

In concluding the meaning of T'ien
or Heaven, the traditional Chinese thought
was that Heaven is the greatest ancester,
also as a religious being in terms of
God in religion.

2.   Chün-tzu

Chün-tzu (君 子) is a highly learned, or a noble type of man, in other
words, a superior man. One of the characteristics in Confucianiasm is to become a superior man through education.
In this regard there is no doubt that
Confucianism is didactic. To Confucius,
human nature is basically good, therefore it is possible to be brought to a
human level, namely to a good citizen
level, and further to a superior man.
The following passages are Confucius'
words about Chün-tzu, a superior man.

子曰, 聖人吾不得而見之矣,
得見君子者, 斯可矣.

Tr. *Confucius said, "I will proba-*
bly not find and see a sage,
but if I see a superior man
it will be alright with me.

子張問善人之道, 子曰, 不踐迹,
亦不入於室.[1]

Tr. 子張 *asked about the way of*
善人 . *Confucius answered:*
*a good man (*善人*) is the one*
who does not blindly follow the
old way, and so he doesn't enter
into the sage's way deeply.

Interpretation: The so-called good man
(善人) is a type of man who does not
blindly follow the old way, therefore

---

[1] 論語, 先進十一.

he is in a distant place from the sage's
place. Thus, a good man (善 人) has
a little creativity of his own.

Also in the next passage, Confucius
said as follows:

子曰，論篤是與，君子者乎，色莊者乎.[1]

Tr. *Confucius said, if a skillful*
    talking is given, is it a
    princely man(君 子) or nice
    looking man(色 莊 者)?

Interpretation: A skillful talker is
often doubtful as to whether he is really a princely man or external only.[1]

子曰，君子，義以為質，禮以行之，
  孫以出之，信以成之，君子哉[2]

---

[1] 論 篤 means a good talking, a
good speaker. 論語, 先進 十一.
[2] 論語, 衛靈公, 第十五, 第十七章.

Tr. *Confucius said; to make
essential with righteous-
ness, to practice in daily
life with propriety, to
bring forth righteousness.
with humility, and to complete righteousness with
sincerity. This is indeed
a superior man.*

子曰，君子求諸己．小人求諸人．[1]

Tr. *Confucius said; a superior
man seeks everything in himself, while a mean man seeks
everything in others.*

子曰，君子不器．[2]

---

[1] 論語．衛靈公．第十五．第二十章．
[2] 論語，爲政．第二，第十二章．

Tr. *A accomplished scholar is not
a utensil.*

子曰，羣居終日，言不及義，

　　好行小慧，難矣哉。[1]

Tr. *Confucius said; if a number
of people are together all
day long without saying, they
are attaining righteousness.
If they are fond of carrying
out a petty cleverness, it is
something hard case.*

子曰，君子矜而不爭，羣而不黨[2]

Tr. *Confucius said; a superior
man is dignified and does not
wrangle. He is sociable, but
not a partisan.*

---

[1] 論語，衛靈公，第十五，第十六章.
[2] ibid. 第二十一章.

3. <u>Jen</u> (亻二)

The meaning of Jen is best expressed as a deep love. Jen is the central
concept in Confucianism just as love in
Christianity. The outskirt of the difference between the two may be deep
love and love. An analytical point of
view for the character 亻二 (Jen) is that
亻 in 亻二 means person or people, and
二 in 亻二 means two. Therefore the
meaning of Jen is a good relationship
between two persons.

In Confucian teaching, Jen is the
central idea and it is antecedent for
Confucianism for both government and
society. Confucius emphasized upon
virtuous government ruled by a virtuous
man, and so was for the feudal society
at that time. The following passages
show Confucius'talks about the meaning
of Jen:

子曰, 巧言令色, 鮮矣仁.[1]

---

[1] 論語, 學而, 第十一, 第三章.

Tr. *Fine words and an insinuating
countenance are seldom associat-
ed with Jen (love, virtue,
deep love).*

子曰, 弟子入則孝, 出則弟, 謹而信,

汎愛眾, 而親仁, 行有餘力,

則以學文.[1]

Tr. *Confucius said; when a youth
is at home, he should be filial.
And when he is with other people outside, he should be respect-
ful to his elders. He should be
earnest and truthful. He should
overflow with Jen (a deep love,
true virtue) to all, and to make
friends of good. If there is
extra time and opportunity, he
should employ them in polite
studies.*

---

[1] 論語, 學而, 第一, 第六章.

顏 淵 問 仁，子曰，克己復禮為仁，
一日克己復禮，天下歸仁焉。[1]

Tr.   *Yen Yuan asked about Jen
(perfect virtue). Confucius
said, to subdue oneself and
return to propriety is perfect virtue. If a man can
subdue himself for one day
and return to propriety, all
under heaven ascribe perfect
virtue to him.*

---

[1] 論語，學而第一，第之章.

II CURRICULUM

A. Wu-lun (五 論 Five
Human Relations)

Wu-lun refers to five human relations. This is an educational theory
promoted by Mencius. The five human
relations are:
    between father and son,
    between ruler and people,
    between husband and wife,
    between older brother and younger
        brother,
    between friends.
Mencius emphasized upon the particular
virtue in each of the relations. That
is, the special virtue between father
and son is filial love and devotion.
The special virtue between ruler and
people is justice and loyalty. The
special virtue between husband and
wife is respect. The special virtue
between older brother and younger brother is submission and humility. The

special virtue of friends is sincerity.

The following is the original passage from Meng-tzu.

后稷教[1]民稼穡[2]，樹蓺五穀
五穀熟而民人育，人之有道也．
飽食煖衣逸居而無教則近於禽獸．
聖人[3]有憂之，使契[4]爲司徒，教以人倫．
父子有親．君臣有義，夫婦有別．
長幼有序．朋友有信．

Tr.   后   稷 *(an official in
agriculture) teaches agriculture
to the people and lets them grow
find grains. When the five grains*

---

[1]后 稷is an official title in Chou
(周) dynasty. In this text, it refers
to the founder of the Chou dynasty 棄 (周
元祖)．
    [2]稼 穡refers to agriculture (to
plant seeds and to grow).
    [3]聖人 in this context refers to
堯舜．
    [4]契 is the name of the founder of
Shang (商) dynasty.

*became ripe, then the people are
nourished. There is the way in
the people [moral behavior]. If
the people eat sufficiently, wear-
ing good and living peacefully
but not being taught, then they
will be close to animals.
The sages (Yao and Shun) were af-
raid of such circumstances, so they
appointed 契 (the founder of Shang
dynasty) as the official of instuct-
ion to teach the people the ethics;
there is filial love and devotion
between father and son. There is
justice and loyalty between ruler
and people. There is a virtue of
respect between husband and wife.
There is submission between older
and younger brothers. And there
is sincerity between friends.*[1]

B. The Six Arts (六 藝)

The six arts were the basic require-
ments for the intellectual level during
the Chou (周) dynasty period, and it

---

[1] 孟子．滕文公．上，第四章

was the basic central curriculum promoted
by Confucius. The six arts were; music _propriety (禮)_
(樂), shooting (射), how to control
horse (御), The Book of History
(書), and Numbers (数). That is to
say, music controls one's feeling. or
mind. Shooting was necessary for hunt-
ing animals for food. To know how to
control a horse was essential for rid-
ing as well as for wheeling carriages. To
know history is still important for
intellectuals. And to know numbers in
terms of the mathematical sense was
also unavoidable. Thus, Confucius
emphasized the six arts for normal education, but it is clear enough from a
number of Confucian documents that
Confucius also emphasized; poetry (詩),
history (書), propriety (禮), and
music (樂) for higher levels which
were assumed to be passed on by the
princely man (Chün Tzu/ 君 子). The following passage is from Chou Li (周 禮)
about the six arts:

大司徒[1] 以鄉三物[2] 教萬民 而賓興之，
一曰六德，知仁聖義忠和，二曰六行，
孝友睦婣任恤，三曰六藝，禮樂
射御書數.

Tr. *The minister of education*
teaches the people with three
instructions [through the local
official]. And selects an ele-
quent one and treats him spe-
cially. First, it is said six
virtues; wisdom (知 *), deep*
love (仁 *), sageness (* 聖 *),*
justice (義 *), loyalty (* 忠 *)*
and peace (和 *). Second, it*
is said six practices; filial
piety (孝 *), friendliness (* 友 *),*
friendly peace with father's side
relatives (睦 *), friendly peace*
*with mother's side relatives (*婣*),*
and trust to friends (恤 *).*

---

[1] 大司徒 is the minister of education in the Chou dynasty.

[2] 三物 refers to three instructions in this text.

Third, it is said the six arts;
propriety (禮), music (樂),
shooting (射), art of driving
chariot (御), history (書),
and Numbers (数).

However, in Lun Yü, Confucius said
when he was fifteen years old, then he
intended to pursue academic works, and
at thirty years of age he became himself. This means that before fifteen
years old, the six arts were mastered.
And after fifteen, poetry (詩), history (書), propriety (禮), and
music (樂) were studied. In a word,
the six arts were the basic require-
ments for the normal intellectuals,
and for an advanced level the classics
were studied. The following is the
original passage from Lun Yü:

子曰, 吾十有五, 而志于學.
三十而立. [1]

---

[1] 論語, 為政.

Tr.   *Confucius said, when I was*
      fifteen, I intended to study
      ·the classics, and when I was
      thirty years old I stood up
      by myself [I was on my own].

The compilation of the above four
classics was initiated by Confucius and
were done in his later life. During the
Ch'in(秦) dynasty, the classics were
burned.. For this reason, some classics
were recompiled such as the Book of
Propriety (禮 記).

C.   Wu Ching (五 経). The Five
     Classics

It is often confusing to identify
the difference between the six arts (六
芸) and the six classice (六 経).
Once again, the six arts were basic
popular curriculum during the Chou dynasty period, promoted by Confucius.
This six arts concept was changed to
the six classics during the Han dynasty
period. The six classics are: The

Book of Poetry (詩經), The Book of
History (書經), The Book of Propriety
(礼經), The Book of Music (樂經), The
Book of Change (易經), and The Annals
of Spring and Autumn (春秋). But in
reality, The Book of Music did not exist,
at least, during the Han dynasty period,
Thus excluding The Book of Music, They
were known as the five classics (五經 /
Wu ching).

Since then, these five classics
became the foundation of Confucianism.
During the period of the T'ang dynasty,
五 經 正 義 (the right meaning of
the Wu Ching). The aim of 五 經
正 義 was to unify the meaning of
each of the classics in terms of the
right meaning.

In this connection, it was popular
among the Confucian scholars to make
notes on the classics. Such an academic atmosphere continued to the Sung
dynasty. However, after the struggling
period of the five dynasties, the
scholars were in general not satis-

fied with making notes on the classics.
Therefore, the scholars had different
speculations, that is, they wanted to
grasp the real meaning directly from the
classics rather than following up the
notes.   Such a trend was initiated by the
Confucian scholars in Northern Sung, and
soon the ideas were synthesized by Chu-
Hsi (朱子) in Southern Sung, and a new
Confucianism emerged, this was known as
the Neo-Confucianism. Since then, Neo-
Confucianism continued to the Yüan and
Ming dynasties.

During the period of Ming under the
Emperor 永樂 , 五經大全 was compiled.
The aim of this book was the right mean-
ing of the classics, which was the same
as 五經正義 compiled during the
T'ang dynasty period. The only difference
was that 五經大全 is based upon the Neo-
Confucian concepts, and mainly on Chu-
Hsi's concepts.

D.   Ssu shu (四書), The Four Books.

The four books are The Great Learning
(大學), Lun Yü (論語), Meng tzu (孟

子) and The <u>Doctrine of Mean</u> (中庸).
Among the four books, 大学 and 中庸
came out of the Book of Propriety (禮
記). 大学 was chapter 42 in the Book of
Propriety and 中庸 was chapter 31 in the
same.   The four books were known since
the time of Chu Tzu (朱子) and Cheng
I-ch'uan (程伊川) in the Sung dynasty.   Both of them were Neo-Confucianists, but their speculations on the traditional Confucianism was different.
They regarded these four books are extremely important, and began to treat
them separately from the five classics,
but as a parallel curriculum for the
higher education. Thus, since the Sung
dynasty on, the four books and the five
classics have been known as 四書五經 .
     However, it may be worthwhile to
note that the Four Books have an order
for study, which was arranged by 程伊
川 while notes were added by 朱子 .
The order is 大学 , 論語, 孟子 ,
and 中庸 . This order is because one
understands a general scope by learning
大学 first, then understands the

fundamentals by learning 論語 ,
then understands the development by
learning 孟子 and then understands
the ancient sages' wisdom by learning
中庸 .

III HISTORICAL DEVELOPMENT

Confucianism is an educational doctrine promoted by Confucius (552-479 B.C.).
Confucius' fundamental idea is "To cultivate oneself, then govern others (修 己
治 人)," on the basis of the deep
love (仁). During the time Confucius
lived, the society in China was chaotic,
that is to say, the states were fighting
each other. For this reason, it was a
natural necessity that some sage must
appear to make the chaotic society into
a peaceful one. Confucius was an official in the state of Lu (魯), but he
left the official position before holding the position long. Thereafter he
became an educator and travelled around
with his disciples. After he came back
to his native state Lu, he taught con-
tinuously and compiled the classics.

Thus, Confucius was the one who
compiled the classics and set up the
educational hierarchy. This means that
the curriculum taught by Confucius was

not initiated by Confucius, but it was
initiated by the previous sages such
as Yao (堯), Shun (舜), Yü (禹),
Tan (湯) and so forth. Under the
chaotic society, Confucius was the one
who emphasized upon returning to the previous sages' teaching for the morality.
But he compiled the classics and set up
the educational hierarchy, that is, the
six arts then the classics. Thus Confucian education was readily generated by
his disciples up to the Ch'ing dynasty.

The following is a passage from
Lun Yü. It shows that Confucius taught
what the previous sages taught:

子曰, 述而不作, 信而好古.
竊比於我老彭. [1]

Tr. *Confucius said, I mention but
I don't create. I trust and
then I like the ancient. I
calmly compare myself with Lao
P'eng (老 彭).*

___

[1] 老彭 (論語, 述而) was a famous official
in Shang dynasty.

Interpretation: Confucius taught what
was good in the past, and trusted those
of good teachings and liked the ancient.
Confucius then calmly compared himself
with Lao P'eng in Yin dynasty because
Lao P'eng was similar to Confucius
himself. That is to say, Lao taught
what his previous sages such as Yao,
Shun, Yü, taught.

Another passage from Chung Yung
is as follows:

仲尼 祖述 堯舜,
憲章文武. (中庸. 第二十九章)

Tr. *Confucius regarded Yao and Shun*
as the greatest ancestral teach-
ers, and taught their virtue,
while keeping the rules of King
Wen (文) and King Wu (武).

Interpretation: Confucius respected
and regarded Yao and Shun as the greatest teachers. What Confucius taught
was what Yao and Shun had taught in
terms of virtue, while Confucius was
keeping the rules of King Wen and King

Wu. That is to say, Confucius taught
what was good in the previous times,
and generated the teachings to his future up to the Ch'ing dynasty. In this
regard, we can see that Confucius'
attitude was conservative.

A. Traditional Confucianism

The traditional Confucianism here
means the Confucianism up to the Sung
dynasty. During this time of Sung, Chu-
hsi (朱 子) and others had a different
point of view about the traditional
Confucianism, and a different theory began to emerge and developed. This later
Confucianism is known as Neo-Confucianism.

The basic difference between traditional Confucianism and Neo-Confucianism is that in the former, the six arts
and the five classics were the basic
curriculum. Of the two, the six arts
were the standard Confucian Curriculum
during Chou (周) dynasty period. The
later, the five classics became the curriculum during the Han dynasty period

until the Sung dynasty, the period in
which Neo-Confucianism emerged. However it is worth noting that the traditional Confucianism was not entirely
succeeded by Neo-Confucianism during
the Sung dynasty, but it developed as
a side line through the Sung dynasty to
the Ch'ing dynasty (清 朝). We will
return to Neo-Confucianism later.

Referring to the traditional
Confucianism, it is the doctrine promoted by Confucius (552-479 B.C.) during the Spring-Autumn period. Confucius
lived in the last part of the Chou dynasty. This was the period that the
traditional social order became chaotic,
and each state was fighting each other.
Under such miserable social circumstances,
it was a heavenly desire that a sage
must appear and make such a society into
a peaceful society. Confucius was a
high official in the state of Lu in his
late life. He left the position because
of a difference of opinions between the
prime minister and himself. Hereafter,
he was travelling around each state with

his thousands of disciples to teach for
peace.

As mentioned earlier, the six arts
are the basic required curriculum for
the Confucian school, but Confucius'
main concept in his heart is the so-
called Jen (deep love). But judging
from his teaching principles, Jen and
Li (propriate) were equally emphasized.
Li is the traditionally prevailing be-
haviorial form in terms of morality,
while Jen can be representative of one's
internal creativity. In other words, Li
constitutes one's behavioral form from
externally just as law does, while
Jen constitutes oneself from his mind,
and the ground of one's mind is based
on ethics.

Confucius' disciples can be largely
divided into two groups. The first
group is those who emphasized Jen, and
they are the subjective people. Those
belonging to this group are 曾子 ,
子思 and 孟子 . The second group
is those who emphasized Li, the objective
group. The notable followers in this

group are 子游 , 子夏 , and 荀子 .

荀 子 was the representative among
those who followed the Li principle.
Later, 荀子 promoted his theory in connection with his Li principle that the
inborn nature of man is bad (性 惡 說).
Therefore, man must be constituted by
law. On the other hand, 孟子 , who
was the representative for those of Jen
who promoted the theory that the inborn
nature of man is essentially good and
that man becomes bad because of social
influence. The legalist's point of
view, after all, helped the unification
of Ch'in (秦) dynasty.

It is interesting to notice that
during the Ch'in dynasty, all the
Confucian classics were burned. This
was because the other group who did not
recognize the legalists' point of view
criticized the government. As the result, it was ordered by the government
to burn all the Confucian classics.
Consequently Confucianism almost died
out. It was not until the former Han
dynasty that Confucianism regained its

development during the Emperor Wu-ti
(武帝). Tung Chung-shu (董 仲
舒) who was a high scholar-official in
the central government advised the Emperor for adoptation of Confucianism as the
national curriculum. The Emperor Wu
accepted Tung Chung-shu's advise, and
set Confucianism as the national curriculum.

Thereafter, all the officials were
busy getting Confucian classics. In
the former time when the Confucian classics were surpressed by the legalists,
some of the classics were hidden in
such places as walls. Now, those classics were found here and there, and the
scholars began to recompile the classics
from the battered pieces. Particularly
Li-Chi, which was the one recompiled
during the Former Han dynasty, and is
available today. Thus, the five classics (wu-ching) appeared during this Han
dynasty period.

In short, the legalists who were
in the line of those who emphasized

Li (propriety) became the end of its
development by the time of Emperor Wu,
and replaced by Confucianism promoted
by those who emphasized Jen. We see
the nature that, at the very beginning,
both schools belonged to the Confucian
school, but gradually those with Li
became the line or legalists while those
with Jen maintained Confucianism all
the way through. Often it is known that
there were originally four different
schools in traditional Chinese thought,
that is, Confucians, Legalists, Universal love, and Taoists. The legalist's
school and the universal love school
were within the realm of Confucian
schools originally, however they were
separated later. Buddhism in China
was much later, it came to China in the
1st centruy A.D.

Now, obtaining the five classics
and studying them was the only way that
man could succeed in terms of getting
government positions.

The characteristic aspect of the
Confucian studies during the Han dy-

nasty period were mainly two types; the
first one was the tendency of specializ-
ing in one of the Confucian classics,
which was popular during the Western Han
period, but it became popular to interpret and to put notes on the whole
Confucian classics during the Eastern
Han period. Thus, the officials were
prepared with Confucian education during
the Han dynasty period. Consequently,
Confucian classics were regarded as
superior to any other classics.

Beginning with the end of the
Eastern Han (東 漢) dynasty to the
Chin (晉) dynasty, the society became
somehow unsettled. Given such an unsettled society, the general atmosphere
of the officials' ideology about Confucian education was also loose, and
there emerged the Taoists' concept, getting gradually more popular. This meant
that Confucianism was weakened during
the six dynasties period. One may often
find Taoists' interpretations and notes
on the Confucian classics during this

six dynasties period. Because of this
trend, the original Confucian teaching
"To cultivate oneself and then rule
others (修 己 治 人)" became secondary teaching. However, this does not
mean that Confucianism was totally
weakened, but it rather means that
Taoist's concept was going on besides
Confucianism. As mentioned, it was popular to interpret and explain the passages
in Confucianism during this six dynasty
period. Another characteristic aspect
of this period was a fixed style of
writing, which was known as four-six
euphuistically antithetic style (Belles
lettres). Like poetic lines, its style
is beautiful, but it limits one's free
expression since one has to follow a
given form in his expression. Soon a
literary movement for free prose writing
emerged.

Han Yü in the T'ang dynasty was a
deep Confucian scholar, and he was one
of the eight prose writers in T'ang and
Sung period. His idea of the literary
movement was to revive the ancient

writings (古 文 復 興). In other
words, his aim of the literary movement
was to return to the ancient free prose
style. Thus, his writings were in free
prose style. He was not only promoting
free prose writing, but also promoted
Confucianism. In one of his essays
"Yüan-tao lun/原 道 論 " he criticized
Buddhism by saying that Buddhism ignores
human ethics, he also criticized Taoism
by saying that Taoism regards the earl-
iest animal-like human life as the
Utopian world.

Han Yü's idea was followed by seven
other literati such as Liu Tsung-Yüan,
Ou Yang-hsiu, and so forth.

In summing up, it can be seen that
up to the early Sung dynasty period the
Confucian education was primarily based
on the traditional Confucianism, and
the interpretations and explanations of
the Confucian classics were the main
atmosphere.

During the Sung dynasty, Chu-tzu
(朱 子) had a speculative idea about

Confucian education, and a new theory
emerged, which was called Neo-Confucianism.

B.   Neo-Confucianism

Neo-Confucianism generally refers
to the metaphysical Confucianism in the
Sung dynasty (960-1127).   In 960 A.D.
Chao K'uang-yin (趙 匡)胤) destroyed
the late Chou (951-960) and founded the
Sung dynasty.   Thereafter for about 100
years, the scholarship was highly developed, and many classics were produced
by the imperial orders.   But these classics were based on the traditional Confucianism in T'ang dynasty, also the
general atmosphere of the education was
nothing more than the inheritance from
that of the T'ang dynasty.   In other
words, there was no particular characteristic from traditional Confucianism.
From such unchanged traditionalism, a
new trend began to emerge.   This new
trend is called Neo-Confucianism.   The
earlier Neo-Confucianism was promoted

by those of Shao K'ang-chieh (邵康節).
Ch'eng Ming-tao (程明道), Ch'eng I-
ch'uan (程伊川), Chang Heng-ch'ü
(張橫渠), etc. in the Northern Sung
(960-1126), but the final hierarchical
theory was by Chu-tzu (朱子) in the
Southern Sung dynasty (1127-1278).

There were two main aspects in the
newly emerging Confucianism. The first
trend was to return to the original
Confucian Texts instead of interpretations or explanations of the classics,
which were done mostly during the Han
and T'ang periods. It was the idea
that the original texts were written or
compiled by Confucius, therefore, the
original texts show the sage's mind
precisely. For this reason, the best
way to understand the sage was a direct
contact to the original texts without
following the interpretations blindly.
Thus, the literary thoughts became quite
different, and it can be seen that there
existed a critical attitude. Also it
is characteristic that the new trend
was not only to return to the original

texts, but to also see the relevant relations to the daily practical life in the Sung dynasty period.

The second trend is the emergence of metaphysics from Confucianism. The metaphysical concept is primarily derived from the idea in the <u>Book of Changes</u> and the <u>Doctrine of Mean</u>. In the <u>Book of Changes</u>, the universality in terms of the ultimate and the two different elements of Yin and Yang are mentioned for the universal structure, and in the <u>Doctrine of Mean</u>, the relationships between nature, way, and instruction (性, 道, 教), also the philosophy of sincerity (誠) was mentioned. The "nature" is mentioned as heavenly order, the "way" is mentioned as obedience, and the "instruction" is mentioned as pursuing knowledge of them. In the later part of the <u>Doctrine of Mean</u>, it is mentioned that the very essential human nature is sincerity. These aspects are the sources that metaphysics in the Sung dynasty is based.

Influence of Buddhism and Taoism.

It is, however, important to understand that the metaphysics in the Sung
dynasty was not only developed from
Confucianism, but great influence was
from Buddhism, and in some extent from
Taoism. The key point in Neo-Confucianism is to understand the term "T'i and
Yung" (体 用), which is originally
derived from Buddhistic logic in terms
of cause and effect. I suppose the
readers of this passage begin to understand what T'i and Yung means in the
logical reasoning in Neo-Confucianism.
However, there are different interpretations about the meaning of T'i and
Yung. In any case, the proper approach
should be to keep in mind something like
"theory and practice, cause and effect,
essence and phenomenon," and so forth.
In other words, T'i is fundamental, and
Yung is derived.

Such a point of view is in accordance to the theory of cause and effect.
Here, it can be seen that cause is some-

thing different from effect, but in Neo-Confucianism T'i and Yung are totally used as a single idea. This means that T'i is Yung and Yung is T'i. It is interesting to notice that in the last part of Ch'ing dynasty (1644-1912), there was a slogan saying "China T'i and West Yung (中 体 西 用)." This means that the education of humanities and social science in China was regarded as T'i, and the natural science and technology in the West is regarded as Yung. Here, one must not confuse that the term is the same, but used in different categories. In this regard I would like to remind those who are concerned with either teaching or learning Neo-Confucianism of the term T'i and Yung. The problem is that should a student learn T'i and Yung in that way in Neo-Confucianism studies, he or she easily turns to nationalism. This is an entirely different approach from the original meaning of T'i and Yung.

In short, in early Confucian classics, it is rare to find T'i and Yung

used in one sense. In other words, each
of the two words is treated separately
for different meaning. In Buddhism,
T'i and Yung are treated as cause and
effect. In Neo-Confucianism, T'i and
Yung are one single meaning, that is,
T'i is Yung and Yung is T'i just like
the concept of being is non-being and
non-being is being. The great universe
consists of everything and everything
consists of the small universe. Thus,
some similarity can be seen in Taoism.

Academic Atmosphere of the Scholar
Gentry.

I have mentioned that Neo-Confucianism is influenced by Buddhism and
Taoism. This means that the scholar
gentry in the Sung dynasty were generally equipped with traditional Confucianism,
Buddhism, and Taoism. Traditional Confucianism emphasizes on ethics, Buddhism emphasizes upon cause and effect, emptiness
and apart from the practical life (出家),
and Taoism emphasizes on no deed but

obedience to the natural course (無 為
自 然). However, it should be
borne in mind that the Sung scholar
gentry were not blindly assimilating
themselves to Buddahism and Taoism.
They were rather relating what were proper to their practical lives from Buddhism and Taoism. In other words, theory
and practice in the light of daily life
is one of the characteristics in Neo-
Confucianism.

Inferring from the general point of
view, the Sung scholar gentry were genuine intellectuals. This means that any
poor peasant could become a member of the
scholar gentry through their studies
and by passing the civil service examination. Generally speaking, the civil
service examination system, which began
during the reign of Emperor Wen (文 帝)
(581-604) in Sui dynasty (隋   ) and
continued until 1905, meant that there
were no inborn social classes which
stopped their way to become a scholar
gentry who were also the leading officials.

However, in reality, those who were
born in poor families did not have a
chance to prepare themselves for the examination. The preparation of the examination normally started at the age of
six or seven years old, but the sons
of poor people could not have enough
chance to prepare for the examination.
This situation implies that the so-called
scholar-gentry were economically and
intellectually upper class people. The
fact was that the officials could have
money because of their good salary,
consequently their sons could also have
good chances to prepare for the civil
service examination, on the other hand,
the poor were always poor, hardly given
a chance to arise. As mentioned, the
officials could have money, but the real
rich people were those who owned land
and their sons had a good chance to come
up to the officials. From such a point
of view, the so-called Shih ta-fu (士
大 夫), scholar gentry, meant those
landlords as well as the scholar. But
it is a misconception to regard the

landlords as the scholar gentry, the
scholar gentry were those of Confucian
scholars and the officials particularly
in the Sung dynasty.

Nevertheless, the civil service examination was officially based upon equality, and there were many cases where one
became a scholar gentry from a low status.
Thus, some historians regard that in
China there was no inborn social class
since the Han dynasty. But close review
of the history indicates that the Han
dynasty society was a heroic society.
Nevertheless those heroes were not
necessarily the scholar gentry. The
scholar gentry were, in fact, those who
graduated from college known as Po-shih
T'i-tzu yüan （博士弟子員 ）. Here
again, it is not considerable that all
the great officials were graduates of
college during the Han dynasty. Following the Han dynasty, the six dynasties'
society was aristocratic, but those
aristocrats were not primarily based
upon scholarly achievement. The priority
was given on the basis of inborn family

lineage. The most representative scholar
gentry during the six dynasties' period
were those who learned the classics known
as Ching-sheng (経 生), but those
Ching-sheng were in general professional
readers of the classics. There were no
such thing that the higher officials
must be in the state of Ching-sheng before they became higher officials.

In comparison with those situations,
the scholar gentry (士 大 夫) in the
Sung dynasty were quite different. The
difference is that the scholar gentry in
the Sung dynasty were based upon scholary
capacity. This means that the higher
officials were members of the scholar
gentry. For the first time, the scholarly capacity and the official positions
coincided. Thus, learning atmosphere
was highly florished.

In fact, the scholarly atmosphere
in harmony with official positions took
place during T'ang dynasty period, but
it was a struggling period between aristocrats and Confucian scholars. Coming
close to the end of the T'ang dynasty,

the aristocratic atmosphere was gone
with an exception of some remains.

The newly established Sung dynasty
society was totally based on scholarly
capacity. This means that the civil
service examination system was based
upon equality. Anyone who prepared for
the examination could take it, and the
examination was the only gate to official positions. Under such flourishing
circumstances, the block-printing became the main medium that distributed
written materials suddenly to every-
where. Out of such rapidly changing
scholarly atmosphere, an emphasis was
given to the difference between the
traditional Confucianism and Neo-Confucianism, besides the consciousness of
agreement and disagreement about Buddhism
and Taoism emerged. Nevertheless, Confucianism was the central force to the
scholar gentry as it dealt with the broad
scope of heaven and man, and Confucianism is concerned with daily practical
life. However, since the scholar gentry

(Confucianists) accepted certain aspects
of Buddhism and Taoism, Neo-Confucianism
means the influence of Buddhism and Taoism to the traditional Confucianism.
Actually, Neo-Confucianism can be considered as the theorization of the com-
bined studies of Confucianism, Buddhism,
and Taoism on the primary ground of the
traditional Confucianism. In this, Neo-
Confucianism deals with Ch'i (氣) and
Li (理), which are related to T'i
(体) and Yung (用). I will return
to T'i and Yung.

In retrospect, the six dynasties
period was an Aristocratic society, consequently the scholar gentry were under
the pressure of the Aristocrats. As
mentioned, it was the T'ang dynasty
period that the so-called power struggle
between Aristocrats and Scholar gentry
emerged, and the Aristocrat power was
swept away, at least, by the end of the
five dynasties period (907-959).[1]

---

[1] This is the five dynasties after
T'ang dynasty, not the one before T'ang
dynasty.

Han Yü and Neo-Confucianism.

After Confucius passed away, Confucianism was developed by his followers
such as Mencius and Hsün-tzu. Mencius
emphasized righteousness and promoted
the idea that man's nature is originally
good but becomes bad by social influence.
Whereas Hsün-tzu emphasized propriety and
promoted the idea that man's nature is
originally bad but becomes good by legal
pressure or propriety. Thus, Hsün-tzu
is known as a legalist.

The legalists held the political
power during the Ch'in dynasty (秦).
One of the high officials, Han Fei (韓
非) began to promote legalism, officialdom, and anticlassicism. The prime
minister Li Ssu (李 斯) accepted the
idea and presented it to Emperor Shih-
huang (221-209 B.C.) in 213 B.C. Then
the Emperor granted, and ordered to burn
the classics except for the records of
the Ch'in dynasty, Books for Medicine,
Books for Agriculture, etc. Also in a
different time, the scholars who were

against the order were captured and received capital punishment.

Coming to the Han dynasty period, the revived Confucianism was overwhelmed by Taoism, and during the six dynasties period Buddhism became popular. Thus, Han Yü, in his Yüan tao （原　道 ） criticized that the original meaning of Jen, I, Tao, and Te （仁義道德、）[1] were all intermingled with Taoism and Buddhism.

Toaists said that Confucius was like a disciple of Lao-tzu, Buddhists also said that Confucius was like a disciple of their Buddha. Han Yü sighed out saying that who could hear the original pure meaning of Jen, I, Tao, and Te. Thus, Han Yü first reviewed the history of Confucianism, and then he mentioned the ancient sage as follows: In the ancient time, many people were bound by obstacles. There, sage appeared and taught them the way to live. It was the

----

[1]Jen is a deep & broad love. I is righteousness in behavior. Tao is to go along with I . Te is one's internal virtue.

sage who became ruler or teacher for the
sake of the troubled people, chasing
away wild and harmful animals and letting
them settle down in the Middle Kingdom.[1]
Setting up rules how to make clothes and
dwellings, choosing technicians and letting them make utensils, choosing merchants for trade, likewise for medicine,
ceremonies, weapons, city wall, etc.
Thus, the ancient sages provided what
was necessary for living. Nevertheless,
Taoists say if the sage does not die,
there is no cease of theft, and if the
peck of dry measure and scale are not
broken, then there is no cease of fighting among the people.[2] But who can
think of such things?

On the contrary, if there was no
sage in ancient times, shouldn't it be
a long time ago that human being died
away because there shouldn't be no even
feather, no one peck of crop to struggle
to get.

---

[1]The Middle Kingdom refers to China:

2 莊子, 胠篋篇.

From this point of view, the scholar
gentry could find a particular characteristic in Confucianism. What is characteristic is the civilization which is given
by the sages. Here we can see the point
that the sages were the creator of civilization.[1] This means that the sages were
creator of rules of propriety such as
ceremonial rules or moral law, and so
forth. Generally speaking, there are
two types of thinking about the term
"Sage" in Confucianism. The one is that
sage was regarded as creator, which was
popular before Neo-Confucianism in the
Sung dynasty. For this reason, the
Duke of Chou (周 公) who was representative as creator was even more highly regarded. In fact, Confucius was conservative, he respected the Duke of Chou
highly. Another type of thinking is that
from the Sung dynasty on, the general concept of sage as creator was changing into the concept that the sage is the one

---

[1]The Book of Propriety describes the
ancient sages as creator (制 作).

who is perfectly equipped with the way
of Jen, I, Tao, and Te (仁 義 道 德),
which was taught by Confucius.

Criticism of Buddhism and Taoism

Han Yü who protected civilization
from the primitive natural way of living
emphasized by Taoists, also protected
the socio-political ethics from Buddhists'
concept. Buddhists emphasize upon de-
parture from secular life in order to be
enlightened. In other words, Buddhists
reject the practical daily socio-political systems. In this, they want to go
to the mountain to live in order to
avoid secular political pressure. In
Buddhists, father is not father, mother
is not mother, and family members are
not family members. At least, they are
not seriously regarded for the fact that
they want to leave family for the mountain. From such point of view, Han Yü
rejects Buddhism just as many people of
those days rejected the theory. An
interesting thing is that Han Yü asserts

one of the passages in the <u>Great Learning</u>
(大学), that is:

> Those who want to brighten the
> ancient virtue to the world,
> should govern the country first;
> those who want to govern the
> country, should rule his family
> first; those who want to rule
> family, should cultivate them-
> selves first; those who want to
> cultivate themselves, should
> rectify their mind first; and
> those who want to rectify their
> mind, should be sincere about
> their ideas.[1]

In spite of this fact, Buddhism, origin-
ated in foreign country instructs
to leave one's country in order to be
enlightened. Thus, destroying ethics;
being a son, who does not treat his
father as father, and being a subject
who does not treat his ruler as the
ruler (In Buddhism, the idea of leaving
the family and going to the mountain
is emphasized). Han Yü further asserts
that Confucius said; those of Chinese
feudal lords who practice foreign pro-

---

[1] 治國, 齊家, 修身, 正心, 誠意.

priety are foreigners. Nevertheless,
Buddhism is highly treated in China.
Is it not strange? Thus, Han Yü was
against Buddhism and promoted Confucianism.

Han Yü was against Taoism also.
Han Yü said "Emperors or Kings are all
sages, only the title is different."
From them comes such knowledge that we
wear thin clothes during summertime,
and feather clothes during wintertime.
In spite of such facts, Taoists emphasize the primitive natural way of
living with no deed to gain something
(無爲自然). This is just like
telling a hungry person who is eating
that why not drinking, and to a person
with feather clothes in winter why
not putting on thin clothes. Thus,
Han Yü was against the primitivism of
Taoists who are against civilization-
ism.

Former Sages' Way.

Han Yü who is against Buddhism and
Taoism mentioned the former kings' way
which he respects and follows. The
former kings' teaching is nothing more
than Jen, I, Tao and Te (仁 義 道 德).[1]
And the literary texts are the <u>Five
Classics</u> (五 經); the law is concerned
with propriety, joy, punishment, and
administration (禮 樂 刑 政); the people
are those of scholars, farmers, artists,
and merchants (士 農 工 商); the human
relations are ruler and subject, father
and son, teacher and student, guest and
master, elder brother and younger brother,
and husband and wife; and clothes, house,
crop, vegetables, meat and fish. These
are very easy instructions to learn and
practice. Therefore, if one applies
these principles to oneself, everything
will be going smoothly. On the other
hand, if one applies these principles
to others, then public love will be
realized. If one applies these prin-

---

[1] See page 56 notes.

ciples to the governance of the country,
things will be proper under heaven.
Such is the way of former kings.

Lineage of Former Sages' Way.

Han Yü then talks about the inheritance of the former kings' way of
saying that the former kings' way is
thus different from Buddhism and Taoism.
The way took place from Yao, and then
was inherited to Shun, from Shun to Yü,
from Yü to T'ang, from T'ang to Wen
Wang, from Wen Wang to Wu Wang, from
Wu Wang to Chou Kung, from Chou Kung to
Confucius, and from Confucius to Mencius.
But after Mencius passed away, the way
was no longer inherited. This passage
is most notable in his Yüan Tao as it
mentions what the former kings' way is.
This way is also known as the sages'
way among Neo-Confucianists. Neo-
Confucianists regard the period between Mencius and Chou Lien-ch'i (周 濂
溪),[1] about one thousand and several

---

[1] 周濂溪 is known as the first
Neo-Confucianist.

hundreds of years, as a dark age because
the former kings' way was not really inherited in a certain sense even though
there were such great Confucianist as
Shun-tzu (苟 子) after Mencius. Historically speaking, the sages were normally following eight people; Yao, Shun,
Yü, T'ang, Wen, Wu, Chou Kung, and
Confucius (Mencius is not normally in-
cluded).

What is the Conclusion of Han Yü   .

Han Yü criticized Buddhism and Taoism because they are apart from practical life. In this sense, if Buddhism
and Taoism are not stopped, Confucianism
cannot be spread out, and the sages' way
cannot be realized. The Buddhist and
Taoist temples must be turned to dwellings for people, otherwise a peaceful
society such as there are no orphans
and no sickened old people cannot be
realized. Such is the main concept of
Han Yü's Yüan Tao. We have the feeling
that Han Yü was the one who revived the

traditional Confucianism in terms of
the former kings' or sages' way. Thus,
Han Yü's <u>Yüan Tao</u> is indeed meaningful
to the development of Neo-Confucianism.

Characteristics in Neo-Confucianism

The Neo-Confucian studies are known
as Tao studies or Sung studies (道学/
宋学). Tao studies <u>here</u> does not
refer to the studies of Taoism. It
strictly refers to Neo-Confucianism in
the Sung dyasty period. The characteristic aspect of these Tao studies is to
bring back the former sages' (kings')
way, which ceased after Mencius for the
period of about 1,400 years until Tao
studies (Neo-Confucianism) emerged during the Sung dynasty period.

As noted earlier, Neo-Confucianism
is characteristic in two aspects. The
first aspect is to pursue the original
Confucian teaching by means of studying the original five classics rather
than derived works such as commen-
taries. Particular emphasis is given

however to Lun Yü, The Great Learning,
The Doctrine of Mean, and Meng Tzu.
Especially "To cultivate oneself, then
to rule family; to rule family successfully, then to govern the country; to
govern the country successfully, then
there is peace under Heaven," in The
Great Learning was mandatory to any
learner. The second aspect is metaphysics or speculative philosophy, that
is, theory was developed, and it was
completed by Chu tzu.

Here again, I would like to talk
about the difference between traditional
Confucianism and Neo-Confucianism. The
traditional Confucianism is concerned
with broad ethics in terms of human relations. Whereas Neo-Confucianism is
concerned with philosophical theory.
For instance, the theoretical relations
of Ch'i and Li (氣 理).

Earlier Pioneers of Neo-Confucianism.

Han Yü (768-824) promoted former
kings' way and Confucius' teaching, but

he was not the one who initiated the
speculative philosophy. For this reason, he is not generally regarded as the
initiator of Neo-Confucionism. The outstanding earlier pioneers of Neo-Confucianism before Chu tzu are; Cho Lien-
ch'i (1017-1073), Ch'eng Ming-tao (1032-
1085), Ch'eng I-ch'uan (1033-1107), and
Chang Heng-ch'ü (1020-1077).

Cho Lien-ch'i is generally known
as the initiator of Neo-Confucianism.
His name is Tun-I (敦 頤) and style
name is Lien-ch'i. He was born in the
province of Hu-nan (湖 南), but later
lived nearby Lu-shan (盧 山). In his
lifetime, Cho Lien-ch'i was unknown,
and he was only a minor official. He
never became a high official. Nevertheless, among his successors are Cheng
Ming-tao and Cheng I-ch'uan who are
brothers. Cho Lien-ch'i became known
after he passed away by the greatest
scholar Chu-tzu who appraised Cho Lien-
ch'i as the scholar. According to Chu-
tzu, Cho Lien-ch'i is the first one
after Mencius who brought back the

original kings' and sages' way. This
means that Chu-tzu regarded the period
of 1,400 years following Mencius as the
dark age that the former kings' and
sages' way was buried.

Cho Lien-ch'i's main idea can be
categorized into four different things:
The first aspect is the diagram repre-
senting the Yin and Yang elements (太
極圖); the second aspect is that one
becomes a sage by learning; the third
aspect is serenity or tranquility (no
desiring of things); and the fourth is
the presentation of Yen-tzu (顏 子),
the beloved disciple of Confucius, and
I-yin (伊尹), a famous minister who
helped King T'an (湯 王) of the Ying
dynasty as the symbolic figure of scholar
gentry.

Ch'eng Ming-tao is generally known
after Cho Lien-ch'i in the promotion and
development of Neo-Confucianism. His
name is Hao (顥) and the style name
is Ming-tao. He was one year older
than his younger brother I-ch'uan. Both

of them studied under Cho Lien-ch'i.
During his earlier days, he was a minor
local official, but later he became a
censor for Emperor Shen-tsung (神 宗).
Shen-tsung favored a progressive policy
supported by Wang An-shih (王 安 石).
Ch'eng Ming-tao was also supporting the
progressive policy initially, but he somehow turned to conservative later. There
he had to leave his official position.
He studied Taoism and Buddhism, but his
main concentration was to seek the right
way in the original Confucian classics,
Wu-ching. His metaphysics were based
upon Ch'i (氣), that is to say, he
presented a new interpretation on the
dual principles of Ying and Yang (nega-
tive and positive). His theory was that
everything in the world was produced
by intermingling with Ying and Yang.
He wanted to unify the duality into
Unitary Ch'i of Heaven. As far as his
ethics were concerned, he regarded bad
or good nature of human as posterior.
This means that human nature is neither

bad nor good originally, but something
comes up in the process of social inter-
actions. However, his teaching was to
cultivate oneself along the line of what
was good or proper. There are not many
of his literary works inherited to to-.
day, but <u>Ting-hsing shu</u> (定 性 書)
and <u>Shih-Jen p'ien</u> (識 仁 篇) are the
primary sources.

 Ch'eng I-Ch'uan was the younger
brother of Ch'eng Ming-tao. He was one
year younger than Ming-tao. I-ch'uan's
name was I (頤) and his style name
was I-ch'uan. The two brothers were
often called Erh Ch'eng-tzu (二程子),
which means the two Ch'eng scholar
gentry. They were only one year different brothers, but their natures were
very different. Ming-tao was so gentle
and kind. Thus, people never saw Ming-
tao when he was angry. I-ch'uan was
stern and an uneasy going person. However, I-ch'uan was appointed as a palace
academic researcher (講 讀 官), and
therefore he had quite a number of dis-

ciples. I-ch'uan was a philosopher, so
he was naturally different from those
who were poetic scholars in literature.
At this time, the outstanding poetic
scholar was Su Shih (蘇 軾) who was
the Hanlin academy (翰 林 院) scholar
(Former college of Literature). I-ch'uan's
followers were called the Lo party (洛
黨) because I-ch'uan was born in Lo Yang
(洛 陽), and Su Shih's followers were
called Shu party (蜀 黨) because Su
Shih was from Shu (蜀 / 四 川). Because of some kind of struggle between
the two parties, I-ch'uan finally had to
leave the official position. Later he
had a chance to come back to the official position, but he was sick and passed away. I-ch'uan's main idea was that
one should not learn the way (Tao) for
something, but one learns the way for
nothing. In other words, one learns
the way in order to understand the way
(Tao) without desiring materials or
honor. I-ch'uan was the first one who
brought out the slogan "to brighten

T'i and to practice Yung (明体達用)."
Among other things, he also presented
the relation between Jen and Ai (仁=愛 /
love), as well as the difference between T'i and Yung, etc.

According to Han Yü in T'ang dynasty, Jen was mentioned as a broad love
in his Yüan Tao. But during the Sung
dynasty period, there emerged various
interpretations about the meaning of
Jen. According to Ch'eng Ming-tao,
Jen consists of righteousness, propriety,
wisdom, and sincerity (義礼智信).
But Chu tzu (朱子) who concluded the
Neo-Confucian theory was holding an
opinion of warning it for the fact that
Chu tzu followed I-ch'uan's theory rather
than Ming-Tao's. I-ch'uan quoted that
Mencius said, "The feeling of commiseration implies Jen (benevolence)[1] and

---

[1] 孟子, 告子章句上, 第六章.
"惻隱之心, 仁也 ---."

commiseration belongs to love." Therefore, people have regarded love as Jen.
Mencius also said "The feeling of commiseration is the beginning of the principle of Jen (benevolence).[1] From such
a point of view, love can be a beginning
of Jen. In other words, love cannot be
a complete Jen. In connection with this
idea, I-ch'uan asserted that love is
a feeling and Jen is nature. Therefore,
love cannot be Jen, at least, in the
immediate sense. Thus, I-ch'uan's theory for Jen was also different from that
of Han Yü who said Jen is broad love.
I-ch'uan's theory for Jen is open equality without privacy, which is substant-
ial to person.[2] And I-ch'uan called
this as T'i in T'i and Yung (体 用)
relations.

---

[1]The works of Mencius (孟子),
公孫丑章句上，茅大章.
"忄則隱之心，仁之端也，"The feeling of commiseration is the beginning of Jen (benevolence).

[2]近思録 2.

Thus, I-ch'uan separated Jen and
Ai. He further mentioned that Jen is
nature (性) which is not actualized
(未 發), and Ai is feeling (情)
which is actualized (已 發). Prob-
ably, what they mean is that the former
refers to a deep human nature, while
the later refers to a sort of visual
surface feeling. This theory was
generated as the following diagram by
Chu-tzu.

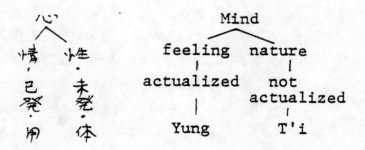

Another outstanding pioneer of Neo-
Confucianism was Chang Heng-ch'ü (1020-
1077). His name was Tsai (載), and
style name was Heng-chü. He was born
in the province of Shensi. His parents
passed away when he was a little boy.
However, his inborn nature was not normal

and he used to talk about military af-
fairs. When he was eighteen years old,
this was the time Li Yüan-hao (李 元
昊) in Tangut (西 夏) often invaded
China. He had a heroic idea to destroy
Li Yüan-hao's army, so he went to the
famous minister Fan Chung-an (范 仲
淹) and expressed himself. Fan Chung-
an then recognized Chang Heng-Ch'ü's
capacity, and told him that he should
learn Confucian teaching rather than
becoming a military leader as the
minister was giving Heng-Ch'ü a book
of The Doctrine of Mean. From this
time on, Heng-ch'ü began to study the
ancient sages' way (道 學).

    Chang Heng-ch'ü's main concept was
the philosophy of Ch'i (氣). Generally speaking in modern Chinese philosophy,
there are three main categories: The
first is "The nature is Li (性 即 理)"
promoted ty I-ch'uan and chu-tzu, which
is known as objective idealism (客 觀
唯 心 論). The second is "The mind is
Li (心 即 理)" promoted by Wang Yang-
ming and Lu Hsiang-shan. This philo-

sophy is known as subjective idealism
（主觀唯心論）. The third is the
philosophy of Ch'i (氣) promoted by
Chang Heng-ch'ü and Wang Fu-chih in
the last part of the Ming dynasty. This
philosophy of Ch'i is known as material-
ism. Chang Heng-ch'ü's main idea was
that the universe is empty (虛). The
extreme apex of the empty is known as
the extreme empty (太虛), which is
nothing more than fullness of Ch'i.[1]
Ch'i is one kind of material, but con-
sisting of Ying and Yang two elements.
The existence of everything in the world
is the process of self-motion of Ch'i.
Thus, everything in the world is born by
the self-motion of Ch'i just as water
becomes ice and ice becomes water. Chang
Heng-ch'ü's idea is that the process of
Ch'i takes a certain way to proceed. In
this regard, the so-called "Tao/the way"
exists. In Chang Heng-ch'ü, birth is a
congelation of Ch'i, and death is a dis-
persion of Ch'i.

---

[1] 正蒙．太和篇．

Chu-Tzu (朱 子 /1130-1200)

Chu-Tzu's real name is Chu-Hsi (朱 熹). He was born in Fu-chien province, but grew up in An-hui province (Chiang- hsi province). His father was a poet and official, who learned Neo-Confu- cianism known as Tao-hsüeh (道 学). The reason that Chu-Tzu began to learn Neo-Confucianism was because of his father's last word. Chu-Tzu is general- ly known as the greatest idealist in Chinese history. His great achievement was the formulation of the hierarchy on Chinese philosophy. His subject cate- gories can be viewed in four aspects. The first aspect is existentialism; the second part is ethics; the third aspect is methodology; and the fourth aspect is the original classics.

As for the existentialism, Chu-Tzu's idea is that Ch'i (氣) is material. when Ch'i is congealed, it produces visual materials, and when it is dis- persed, it is invisible just as moisture and water or water and ice. Chu-Tzu,

however, asserts that basically there
is only one Ch'i, but through its
self-motion, it produces Ying and Yang
two elements. From the Ying, gold (金)
and water (水) are produced by congelation; and from Yang tree and fire are
produced in the same manner. Besides
these four elements, there is one more
element, which is soil. This soil element exists among the four elements as
a sort of core, and acts as making the
four elements into their own characteristics. This means if there is
no soil, the four elements cannot exist
respectively. And from the five elements (五 行), everything is produced
by respective congelation. In a word,
Ch'i is a basic material, which produces
Ying and Yang. Ying and Yang produce
the five elements, and the five elements
produce everything.

     In regard to Chu-Tzu's ethics, Chu-
Tzu emphasizes that "Nature is Li" (性
即 理). This is the main body in Neo-
Confucianism. To Chu-Tzu, nature (性)

belongs to Li (理), not to Ch'i (氣).
In regard to the relation between Ch'i
and Li, there were serious arguments
among the contemporary philosophers
with Chu-Tzu. Generally speaking, Ch'i
is material fulfilled in the universe,
while Li is in respective individual
things. But the important thing is that
Li is not material, but it is rather a
deep principle that an individual thing
should come to exist, instead an individual thing merely comes to exist.
Here, we can predict that principle
means a heavenly order in ethics and
in nature. The diagram in the following page shows Chu-Tzu's theory on
ethics.

    In regard to the meaning of T'i
and Yung (体 甩), there was no
agreement. Some philosophers regarded
T'i and Yung as an equal meaning. Some
regarded them differently. As far as
the terminology is concerned, it is rare
in Confucian classics before the Sung
dynasty. However, they appear sparsely.

Chu-Tzu's Theory on Ethics

Surface/ Appeared	用	Deep/Heavenly Essence	体
Material Substance	氣	Principle law of nature	理
Materialism	形而下	Metaphysics	形而上
Utensil	器		
Initiated	已發	Disposition of Providence	道
Mild	和		
Dynamic	動	Not Initiated	未發
		Inside	中
		Static	靜

The heart
心

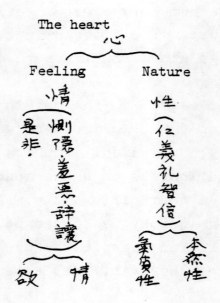

Feeling   Nature

It is in Buddhist texts that they appear
rather frequently in connection with
"cause and effect" relations. For this
reason, it is often thought that T'i and
Yung terminology came from Buddhism. In
any case, one should keep in mind that
T'i is something innermost ethical essence,
while Yung is something appeared.

In regard to Chu-Tzu's method for
cultivating oneself to be a sage, he
emphasized two aspects; one was to respect the nature of virtue (居 敬), and
the other was to advance one's studies
(窮 理 / 格 物 致 知). What Chu-Tzu
meant by "To respect the nature of virtue"
was to concentrate upon one thing to arrive at the original heavenly nature.
And "To advance one's studies" meant to
investigate things throughly and extend
one's knowledge to the utmost. We can
think of this as such by knowing past
and present things throughly, our knowledge can be extended to other things as
well as to future problems. Chu-Tzu
regarded "To investigate things" as "To

investigate problems."

The fourth aspect that Chu-Tzu emphasized is the studies on the original
Confucian Classics. He emphasized on the
original works because this is the direct
access to the former Sages' way. Chu-Tzu
particularly emphasized upon the Four
Books (四 書). These are <u>Confucian
Analects</u> (論 語), <u>The Great Learning</u>
(大 學), <u>The Doctrine of Mean</u> (中 庸),
and <u>The Works of Mencius</u> (孟子). Out
of these four books, <u>Ta Hsüeh</u> and <u>Chung-
Yung</u> were from <u>Li-Chi</u>. Each of the two
books were originally two chapters in <u>Li
Chi</u>,[1] but Chu Tzu saw these two chapters
were extremely important to the Neo-
Confucianism, so he took out the two
chapters and made them separate books.
The so-called four books and five classics (四 書 五 經) means these four
books in the Sung dynasty and the original five classics, that is: <u>The Book of</u>

---

[1] <u>Ta Hsüeh</u> is chapter 42 in <u>Li Chi</u>,
<u>Chung-Yung</u> is chapter 31 in <u>Li Chi</u>. <u>Li
Chi</u> is the <u>Book of Rites</u>.

Changes, The Book of Odes, The Book of
History, The Book of Rites, and The
Spring and Autumn Annals. (易經,
詩經, 書經, 禮經, 春秋).
    As mentioned, the four books were
particularly emphasized, but there were
other classics promoted by Chu-Tzu also.
    I have mentioned Chu-Tzu's four
main ideas. Other than these four characteristics, Chu-Tzu was also favored
in his opinion on the Civil Service
Examination policy, agricultural promotion policy, and so forth.

IV   THE EFFECTS AND CRITICISM

The basic difference between Confucianism and Taoism is that Confucianism
is concerned with the practical world
in terms of human relations and government policy. Whereas Taoism is not concerned with human relations neither ethics nor government, but concerned with
submission to nature. However, during
the Warring period, Confucianism was one
of the few socio-political ideas. It was
during the Han dynasty period that Emper-
or Wu (Wu Ti) recognized Confucianism
as the national curriculums. Thus, Confucian studies began to dominate, and
during the Sui dynasty period the civil
service examination took place. Thereafter, the examination system continued
until the end of the Ch'ing dynasty with
a short period of hiatus in the early
part of the Yüan dynasty. This means
that for one thousand three hundred years,
the examination system continued, which
made Chinese culture deeply rooted to

Confucianism. Thus, Confucianism certain-
ly served for unifying Chinese culture,
but the textual criticism began to emerge
during the Ch'ing dynasty period. The
criticism was mainly for the following
reasons: (1) Lack of creativity, (2)
The impact of the civil service examination, and (3) The prohibitive of the
development of natural science.

A.   Lack of Creativity

Generally speaking, Chinese culture
is on the grounds of realism. This is
because Confucianism dominated the society,
and Confucianism is concerned with the
practical world. In other words, it
taught how humans should behave in terms
of ethics, whereas Taoism and Buddhism
escaped from the practical world. Since
Confucianism became the national curriculum, moreover, it became the subject
for the civil service examination, people
had to learn and practice what Confucius
said. Now, let me bring out a passage in
Lun Yü. Confucius said:

子曰, 述而不作, 信而好古.
窃比於我老彭. [1]

Tr.   *Confucius says, propagate the*
       Ancients and not to create.
       Trust and love the Ancients.
       Calmly compare myself with
       Lao P'eng. [2]

Interpretation: Confucius says, learn
and propagate what the Ancients said because past civilization is the cumulation
of human wisdom, and don't create anything because creation is any sort of
one's own doing. But to learn Ancients
does not mean to learn everything in the
past, it means to trust trustful things
and appreciate the ancient civilization.
This is my attitude, however it is not
only in my case. There was Lao P'eng, a
famous Ying dynasty official who thought
this way also.

---

1 論語, 述而.

[2]Lao P'eng (老 彭) was a famous
politician during Ying (Shang) dynasty.
古注 (Explanatory notes, Han dynasty) by 包子.

From the standpoint of the above passage, we can notice that Confucianism does not assert creativity. The fact is that creativity is necessary, for literature such as fiction, also no natural science can be developed without creativity. This is one of the main reasons understood to the general literati why the development of natural science in China is behind.

B.   The Impact of Civil Service
Examination

The civil service examination took place during the Sui dynasty. It is most characteristic that to be a high official in the government, one must pass the examination. Thus, the central political system and the employment of officials by means of the examination were unseparable. The following are the aspects which did not promote natural scientific development: (1) The basic philosophy of the examination, (2) A brief historical outline. (3) The contents of the examination. (4) Preparation of the examina-

tion.   (5) Privilege of those who passed
the examination.

a. The Basic Philosophy of the Examina-
    tion.

     In regard to the applicants of the
examination, it was not limited to the
privileged class, but open to everyone.[1]
However, poor people never had the chance
to prepare themselves for the examination.
The examination subjects were three categories; the first was the translation
and interpretation of the Confucian classics, not any other classics, the second
was about political history and politics,
and the third was about composing poetry.
All of these subjects were from Confucian
classics, so there was no need to study
any other classics. It is, however,
notable that law was not taken as the
examination subject. The answer for the
examination had to be in the style of the
eight-legged essay (八 股 文).

---

[1] Only man was allowed to be the applicant. However, a low-down businessman
was not allowed to be an applicant.

b. A Brief Historical Outline

Before the mid part of the Late Han dynasty, officials were customarily select- ed by community people. But beginning from the mid part of the Late Han dynasty, the local powerful families were expand- ing their power and gradually entered into officialdom. For this reason, during the Wei Kingdom (220-264),[1] the central govern- ment established a new system called "Se- lection of nine classes' officials" (九品 官人法 / 九品中正法). This new system was that the central government appointed a local official known as up- right official (中正官) to a local district to investigate talent of the applicants for official positions, and the official had the right to classify the applicants into nine levels. The official then reported the classifi- cation to the central government. The central government maintained a table of nine classes' officials (九品官判表).

---

[1]Wei Kingdom; one of the three kingdoms founded by Ts'ao Ts'ao.

and according to the table of organiza-
tion, officials were appointed.

The effect of this system soon
turned out that no matter how many upright
officials there were in a given district,
it was not possible to select genuine
quality among the applicants. Very often,
the applicants were selected from powerful families again, and the officialdom
became hereditary toward aristocracy.

So far, there was no civil service
examination system. It was during the
Sui dynasty period that the civil service
examination system was established. The
Sui dynasty reformed the local districts
on a large scale, and it became effective
that over-all officials were appointed
by the central government. For this
reason, the government needed a large
number of officials. This became the
reason for the implementation of the
civil service examination system. As the
result of the examination system, aristocracy collapsed.

c. The Contents of the Examination.

The main category of the civil service examination can be divided into
three parts: (1) Local examination, (2)
Capital examination and, (3) Palace examination. Each dynasty had different
systems, but approximately as follows:

The local examination consisted
of three levels: Hsien-shih (县 試)
limited to five times, Fu-shih (府 試)
limited to three times, Yüan-shih(院
試) limited to four times. After these
examinations, successful candidates became Sheng-yüan (生 員 /degree).

After Sheng-yüan there were two
levels for the next degree: K'o-shih
(科 試) limited to once, and Hsiang-
shih (鄉 試) limited to three times.
A successful candidate became Chü-jen
(举 人 / 2nd degree).

After this Chü-jen degree, there
were four levels: Chü-jen fu-shih (举
人 覆 試) limited to once, Hui-shih
(会 試) limited to three times, Hui-

shih fu-shih (今 試 覆 試) limited
to once, Tien-shih (殿　試) limited to once. A successful candidate then
became Chin-shih (進 士 / 3rd degree).

　　After the Chin-shih degree, there
was one level called Chao-kao (朝 考)
limited to once. A successful candidate
then became Shu-chi-shih (庶 吉 士 / 4th
degree). After Shu-chi-shih, there was
another examination called San-kuan kao-
shih (散 館 考 試) for those who
failed to reach high appointments among
the Hanlin graduates (翰 林 院).

　　As mentioned, the examination subjects were in three fields: The first
was interpretation of Confucian classics,
the second is politics, and the third is
about poetry. All the subjects must be
based on Confucian classics, and the examination answer must be in the style of
the eight-legged essay (八 股 文). Again
noticing that there were no natural science subject for the examination.

d. <u>Preparation for the Examination</u>

The preparation for the examination
began as early as five or six years old.
The method of study for the Confucian
classics was memorization of passages,
and the family normally employed a tutor,
to whom they had to pay a good reward.
For this reason, poor people could hardly
initiate the preparation.

e. <u>Privilege of Those Who Passed the
Examination</u>.

Those who passed the examination
could become high officials and therefore
become rich because of the good salary.
So, to pass the examination and to become a high official means not only for
the individual who passed the exam, but
equal status of family as well as one's
relatives.

C. The Reason Why Natural
Science was not Developed

In regard to the reason why natural

science was not developed, the following
aspects are considered: (1) Natural
science was not the subject that concerned the officials. (2) The classifica-
tion of the classics, (3) Apart from
practical education, (4) The Chinese
cultural thought (中 華 思 想), and (5)
the influence of Ying-Yang concept.

a. Natural Science was not the Subject
That Concerned the Officials.

The civil service examination was
the only means to become a high official
for 1,300 years since the examination
system was established during the Sui
dynasty. The subject matter for the
examination was only concerned with three
fields; Confucian classics, Politics, and
the composing of poetry. All of these
subjects were based on Confucianism, there
was nothing for the natural science subject. For this reason, there was no way
that natural science could be developed.

b. <u>The four classifications</u>

The over-all literary works were classified into four categories; the first part is for the classics (経部), the second part is for historical works, the third part is for various philosophers' works, and the fourth is for the collection of literature. However, some natural science works are collected in the philosophers' section such as agriculture, medical science, mathematics and astronomy. From the standpoint of these four classifications, one can notice that there were no emphasis on natural science.

c. <u>Apart from Practical Education</u>

Generally speaking, the traditional Chinese education was for the sake of the ruling class in order to rule people. The ruler is son of Heaven (天子), and the loyalty of the people to their ruler was the primary education. Furthermore, emphasis was given to memorization of sages' passages, not individual's creativity. It is indeed doubtful as to what

extent such memorization became effective
to the practical life.

d. <u>Chinese Cultural Thought</u> (中華 思 想.).

It is generally known that Chinese
nationality is conservative and oldish.
When a given Chinese person encounters
a difficulty, he thinks the problem-solv-
ing key is in the classics because Chinese
people normally think Chinese classics
maintain all kinds of difficulty-solving
policies. Such thought can be regarded
as Chinese cultural thought (中華 思 想.).
In other words, it means China is in
splendor, and the surrounding countries
are secondary. Consequently, Chinese
people hardly learned foreign cultures.

Historically, such cultural thought
was encountered with difficulties toward
the end of the Ch'ing dynasty when the
officials saw the advanced Western science and technique through the Western
military activities. This was the time
that the Chinese officials began to build
various military factories and began to

import Western technology. Then, the slogan was "Chung-T'i Hsi-Yung" (中体西用).
This refers to the superiority of the
spiritual culture in China, while promoting the idea of learning Western
technology for the sake of utilization.
Furthermore, it was quite popular that
the origin of the Western academy was
contained in the Chinese classics. This
implies that to import Western technology
into China is what ought to be done.

Even today, many Chinese nationals
have such traditional Chinese thoughts,
which is one of the factors why natural
science is behind in its development

e. The influence of Ying-Yang
What are most characteristic in
the Chinese academy are the studies of
Confucian classics and ethics in terms
of the emphasis on Jen (仁), Li (禮),
Yi (義), and so forth. These terms are
abstract, but constitute ideal discipline.

There were no such studies as analyzing
material to see concrete phenomena in
natural science. On the contrary, Chinese
scholars often relied upon intuition or
direct knowledge. And the intuitive knowledge is based upon either past experience
or on the ideas such as Ying-Yang in the
Book of Changes or the five elements.
Here, I would like to say again that the
concrete material analyses in natural
science is in opposition to the intuitive
approach.

f.   Lack of Theory and Practice.

Another aspect that I would like to
point out is the lack of theory and practice in daily life. However, it has been
coincided with practice in the field of
ethics and political hierarchy, but not
in the field of material production,
namely natural science. As early as the
Sung dynasty, Chu-Tzu presented Ch'i as
material in the air, related to atomic
energy today, but it was not developed.

V CONCLUSION

I have tried to respond to the intellectual question of what Confucianism
and Neo-Confucianism are and why Confucianism is criticized. My response was
that the traditional Confucianism is
based upon socio-political ethics. Neo-
Confucianism also emphasizes ethics, but
most characteristic aspects are speculative philosophy in terms of the hierarchy of T'i and Yung categories.

However, Confucianism was criticized
in the later period on the ground that
it lacks creativity in the sense of
natural science development. My point
of view is that if we consider Confucianism as social science, humanities and
ethics, I do not see anything wrong with
Confucianism even in the light of modern
days. Even today, students need to imi-
tate their teachers in many fields of
study such as language learning without
being creative. However, it appears

important how to interprete the original
Confucian passages since every passage
covers a deep and broad meaning.

Another point is that Confucianism
did not stop natural scientific development, but it was the civil service examination system which was soley based
upon Confucianism, no other subjects.
Consequently, no one studied any other
subjects than Confucianism to be a high
official. For this reason, natural science was disregarded. The responsibility
for the underdevelopment of natural science is due to the high officials who
controlled the civil service examinations,
not Confucianism. As mentioned above,
Chu-Tzu in the Sung dynasty presented
Ch'i (气) as material in the air,
closely related to atomic energy, but
it was not developed. Tracing back to
Chinese society, paper, compass, and
explosion powder discoveries were far
earlier than that of any other parts of
the world in spite of a heavy pressure of
the social science.

I believe that the delay of natural
science development in China was not
caused by Confucianism, but it was caused
by the subject matter in the civil service examination. In other words, there
was no natural science subjects involved
in the examination system throughout
Chinese history. The responsibility must
be assumed to the high officials for the
delay of natural science development, not
Confucianism itself. In fact, Confucianism brought civilization in China.

	Name	Time	Description
1	孔丘	春秋	字仲尼
2	孔鯉	春秋	字伯魚. Son of Confucius. Died earlier than Confucius at the age of 50.
3	孔伋	戰國	字子思. Son of 鯉. Disciple of 曾子.
4	孔白	戰國	字子上. Son of 伋. He was offered a minister position by the King 威王 of Chi (齊), but he did not accept the position. Died at the age of 47.
5	孔求	戰國	字子家. Son of 白. The King of Ch'u (楚) invited him, but he did not accept the invitation.
6	孔箕	戰國	字子高. Son of 箕. He became a minister of Wei (魏). Died at the age of 46.
7	孔穿	戰國	字子高. Son of 箕. He wrote 讕言 十二篇. Died at the age of 51.
8	孔謙	戰國	字子順. Son of 穿. He became a minister under the King 安釐 of 魏. Died at the age of 57. He had three sons; the first one was called who wrote 孔叢子二十一篇. The second son was called 騰, and the third was called 樹.
9	孔騰	前漢	字子襄. The second son of 謙. He became 博士 at the time of King 惠帝. Died at the age of 57.
10	孔忠	前漢	字子貞. Son of 騰. He became 博士 during the reign of 文帝. Died at the age of 52.
11	孔武	前漢	字子威. Son of 忠. He became 博士 during the reign of 文帝.
12	孔延年	前漢	Son of 武. He became 博士 during the reign of 武帝. Died at the age of 71.

13	孔霸	前漢	字次孺 . Son of 延年 . He became 博士 during the reign of 昭帝 . Also he held high official positions. Died at the age of 72.
14	孔福	前漢	Son of 霸 . He was 關內侯 under the Emperor 成帝 . Died at the age of 62.
15	孔房	前漢	Son of 福 . He was 關內侯 under 哀帝 .
16	孔均	前漢	字長平 . Son of 房 . He became the prime minister during the time of 王恭 .
17	孔志	後漢	Son of 均 . He was 大司馬 during during the reign of 光武帝 .
18	孔損	後漢	字君益 . Son of 志 . He became 褒亭侯 during the reign of 明帝 .
19	孔曜	後漢	字君曜 . Son of 損 . He had two sons; the first one was called 完 , and the second was called 讚 .
20	孔完	魏	Son of 曜 . He was 襃亭侯 . Died in his early age and he did not have son. The Emperor 文帝 appointed 羨 who was the son of 完's younger brother 讚 to succeed 完's duty.
21	孔羨	魏	字子餘 . He became 宗聖侯 during the reign of 文帝 of Wei (魏) .
22	孔震	魏 晉	字伯起 . Son of 羨 . He became 崇聖侯 , and he was also 奉聖亭侯 during the reign of 武帝 of 晉
23	孔嶷	晉	字成功 . Son of 震 . 奉聖亭侯 . Died at the age of 57.
24	孔撫	晉	Son of 嶷 . 豫章太守 .
25	孔懿	晉	Son of 撫 . 奉聖亭侯 and 從事中郎 .

26	孔群	南业朝	字群之． Son of 壹忿 ．奉聖亭侯 and 崇聖侯．
27	孔乘	南业朝	字敬山． Son of 群． 崇聖太夫．
28	孔靈珍	南业朝	Son of 乘． 崇聖侯 under 孝文帝．
29	孔文泰	南业朝	Son of 靈． 崇聖侯． Died at the age of 58.
30	孔渠	南业朝	Son of 文泰． 崇聖侯．
31	孔長孫	南业朝	Son of 渠． 崇聖侯． Died at the age of 64.
32	孔嗣悊	隋	Son of 長孫． 紹聖侯 under the Emperor 煬帝 of 隋．
33	孔德倫	唐	Son of 嗣悊． 襃聖侯 during the reign of 高祖 of 唐．
34	孔崇基	唐	Son of 德倫． 襃聖侯 under 中宗．
35	孔璲之	唐	字藏暉． Son of 崇基．襃聖侯． An Lu-Shan revelion in his time.
36	孔萱	唐	Son of 璲之． 文宣公． 兖卅泗水令．
37	孔齊卿	唐	Son of 萱． 文宣公．
38	孔惟晊	唐	Son of 齊卿． 文宣公 under 德宗
39	孔策	唐	Son of 惟晊． 文宣公 under 武宗．
40	孔振	唐	字國文． Son of 策． 進士． 秘書省校書郎．文宣公． Died at the age of 60.
41	孔昭儉	唐	Son of 振 ．兖卅司馬． 秘書郎． 文宣公 ．曲阜令．
42	孔光嗣	唐	Son of 昭儉． He was appointed as 泗水主簿 by the Emperor 昭宗， but was killed by a man right after the appointment.

43	孔仁玉	五代	字温如 。 Son of 光嗣 。 文宣公 at the time of 後唐 , and 曲阜令 at the time of 後晉 , also 監察御史， 兵部尚書 under 太祖 of 後周 。
44	孔宜	宋	字不疑 。 Son of 仁玉 。 曲阜主簿，齊州防禦推官，司農寺丞，太子右贊善大夫，封爵。
45	孔延世	宋	字茂先 。 Son of 宜 。 曲阜令 ， 文宣公 。
46	孔聖佑	宋	Son of 延世 。 文宣公 。 He did not have son.
47	孔宗愿	宋	字子莊 。 Son of 延澤, who was younger brother of 延世 (45). 國子監主簿，文宣公，衍聖公 。
48	孔若蒙	宋	字公明 。 Son of 宗愿，衍聖公 。
49	孔若虛	宋	字公實 。 衍聖公 。
50	孔端友	宋	字子交 。 Son of 若虛。衍聖公 。
51	孔玠	宋	Son of 端操 , who was the younger brother of 端友 (50). 衍聖公 。
52	孔璠	金	Younger brother of 玠 (51) and the second son of 端操。 衍聖公 。
53	孔搢	宋	字季紳 。 Son of 玠 。 衍聖公 。
54	孔拯	金	字元齊 。 Son of 璠 。 衍聖公 。
55	孔摠	金	字元會 。 Son of 璠 , and younger brother of 拯 。 衍聖公 。
56	孔文遠	宋	字紹先 。 Son of 搢 。 衍聖公 。
57	孔元措	金	字夢得 。 Son of 摠 。 衍聖公 。
58	孔萬春	宋	字耆年 。 Son of 文遠 。 衍聖公 。
59	孔湞	金	字昭度 。 Grandson of 元紘 who was the younger brother of 元措 。 衍聖公 。

60	孔沫	宋	字景清. Son of 嵩香. 衍聖公.
61	孔治	元	字世安. A descendant of 若虛 (49) in six generations. 衍聖公.
62	孔思晦	元	字明道. A descendant of 若愚 in seven generations. 若愚 was the younger brother of 若虛 (49).
63	孔克堅	元	字璟夫. Son of 思晦. 同知太常禮儀院事.
64	孔希學	明	字士行. Son of 克堅. 衍聖公. Died at the age of 47.
65	孔訥	明	字言白. (son of 希學?). 衍聖公.
66	孔公鑑	明	字昭文. Son of 訥. 衍聖公. Died at the age of 23.
67	孔彥縉	明	字朝紳. Son of 公鑑. 衍聖公. Died at the age of 55.
68	孔承慶	明	字永祉. Son of 彥縉. 衍聖公.
69	孔宏緒	明	字以敬. Son of 承慶. He became a high official (爵), but lost the position. (see 70).
70	孔宏泰	明	字以和. Second son of 承慶. He became a high official (爵) by succeeding his elder brother's position.
71	孔聞韶	明	字知德. Son of 宏緒. He was 爵.
72	孔貞幹	明	字用濟. Son of 聞韶. 衍聖公. Died at the age of 38.
73	孔尚賢	明	字象之. Son of 貞幹. 衍聖公. Died at the age of 78.
74	孔衍植	清	字懋甲. Grand son of 貞寧 who was the younger brother of 貞幹 (72).

75	孔興燮	清	字起呂。 Son of 衍植。衍聖公。
76	孔毓圻	清	字鐘在。 Son of 興燮。衍聖公。
77	孔傳鐸	清	字振路。 Son of 毓圻。衍聖公。
78	孔繼濩	清	字體和。 Son of 傳鐸。衍聖公。
79	孔廣棨	清	字京立。 Son of 繼濩。衍聖公。 Died at the age of 31.
80	孔昭煥	清	字曝明。 Son of 廣棨。衍聖公。 Died at the age of 47.
81	孔憲培	清	字養元。 Son of 昭煥。衍聖公。 Died at the age of 58.
82	孔慶鎔	清	字治山。 Son of 憲增 who was the younger brother of 憲培(81).
83	孔繁灝	清	字文淵。 (son of 慶鎔)。 衍聖公，太子太保。
84	孔祥珂	清	字觀堂。 (son of 繁灝)。
85	孔令貽	清 民國	字燕庭。 Died in the 8th year of Republic of China (民國)。
86	孔德成	民國	字達生。 (son of 令貽)。 He was born in the 9th year of Republic of China (民國)。

BIBLIOGRAPHY

Alexander, G.G., Confucius, the Great
    Teacher, London, 1890.

Brown, Brian, The Story of Confucius,
    His Life and Sayings, Philadelphia,
    1927.

Carus, Paul, Chinese Thought, Chicago,
    1907.

Chan, Wing-tsit, An Outline and a
    Bibliography of Chinese Philosophy,
    Hanover, New Hampshire.

Chen, Huan-chang, The Economic Principles
    of Confucius and His School. 2 vol.,
    N.Y., 1911.

Cheng, Tien-hsi, China Moulded by
    Confucius, London, 1946.

Collis, Maurice, The First Holy One,
    N.Y., 1948.

Creel, H.G., Confucius, the Man and the
    Myth, N.Y., 1949.

Creel, H.G., Sinismi A Study of the Evolu-
     tion of the Chinese World View,
     Chicago, 1929.

Crow, Carl, Master K'ung, the Story of
     Confucius, N.Y., 1938.

Dawson, Miles. Ethics of Confucius,
     N.Y., 1915.

Dubs, Homer H., "The Dates of Confucius'
     Birth," Asia Major, N.S.I., Pt.
     II, London, 1949.

Faber, Ernest, A Systematic Digest of
     the Doctrines of Confucius (trans.
     by P.G. Von Mollendorff), Shanghai,
     1902?

Fung Yu-lan, A History of Chinese Philo-
     sophy (trans. by D. Bodde), 2 vol.,
     Princeton, 1925-3.

Fung Yu-lan, A Short History of Chinese
     Philosophy, N.Y., 1948.

Fung Yu-lan, The Spirit of Chinese Philo-
     sophy (trans. by E.R. Hughes),
     London, 1947.

Giles, Herbert A., Confucianism and Its Rivals, London, 1915.

Starr, Frederick, Confucianism, N.Y., 1930

Wilhem, Richard, Confucius and Confucianism, (trans. by George E. Danton and Annina P. Danton), N.Y., 1931.

Waley, Arthur, Three Ways of Thought in Ancient China, London, 1939.

Confucian Classics

Chen, Ivan, The Book of Filial Piety, London, 1908.

Hughes, E.R., The Great Learning & the Mean-in-Action, London, 1942.

Kramers, Robert Paul, K'ung Tzu Chia Yü; the School Sayings of Confucius, Lieden, 1949.

Legge, James, The Chinese Classics, 5 vols. in 8, Hong-Kong, 1861-72. Vol. 1. "The Prolegomena"; Confucian Analects; The Great Learning; The Doctrine of the Mean.

Vol. 2.   The Works of Mencius.

Vol. 3.   The Shoo King; or, The
Book of Historical Documents.

Vol. 4.   The She King: or, The Book
of Poetry.

Vol. 5.   The Chun Tsen (Spring and
Autumn), with the Tso Chuen
(Tso's Commentary).

Lin Yutang, The Wisdom of Confucius,
N.Y., 1938.

Waley, Arthur, The Analects of Confucius,
N.Y., 1939.

Waley, Arthur, The Book of Songs,
London, 1937.

Wilhelm, Richard, The I Ching or the
Book of Changes, N.Y., 1950.

INDEX

DATE DUE

HIGHSMITH   #LO-45220